The best cake

Story by Beverley Randell
Illustrated by Naomi Lewis

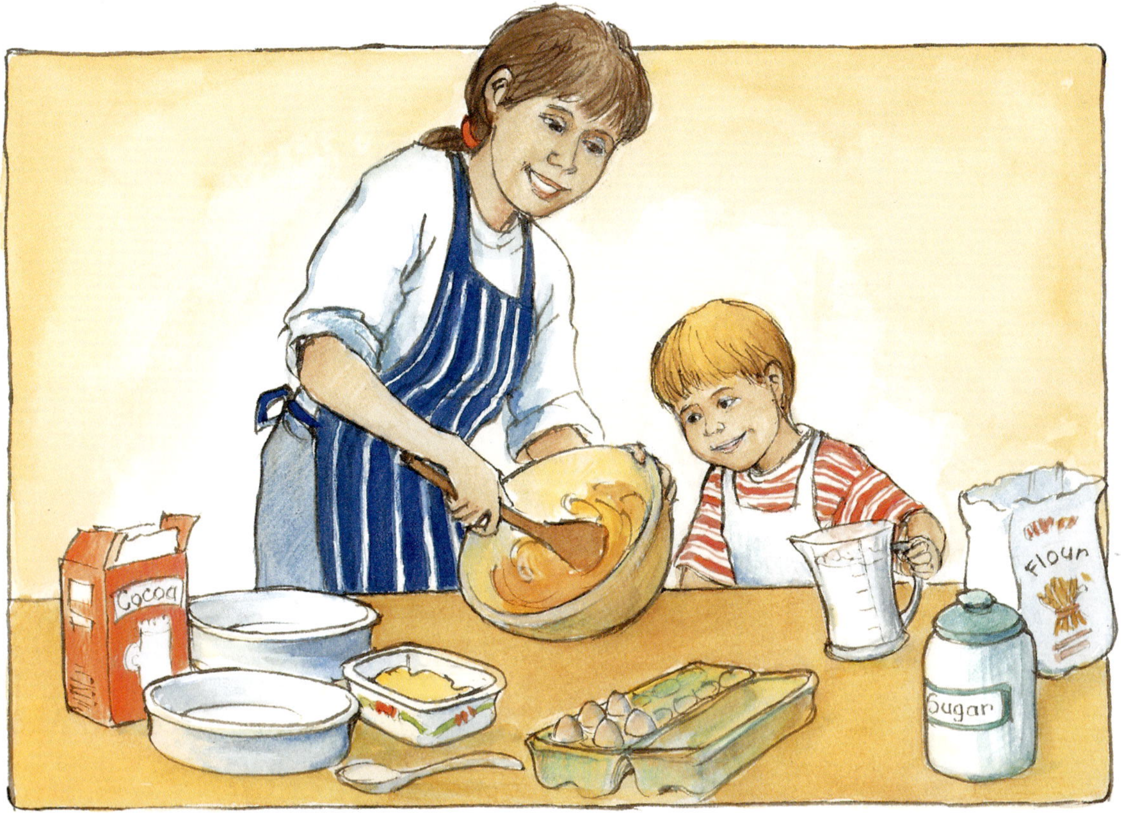
Cocoa
Flour
Sugar

Ben liked making cakes.
He helped Mom
make a cake
for the school fair.

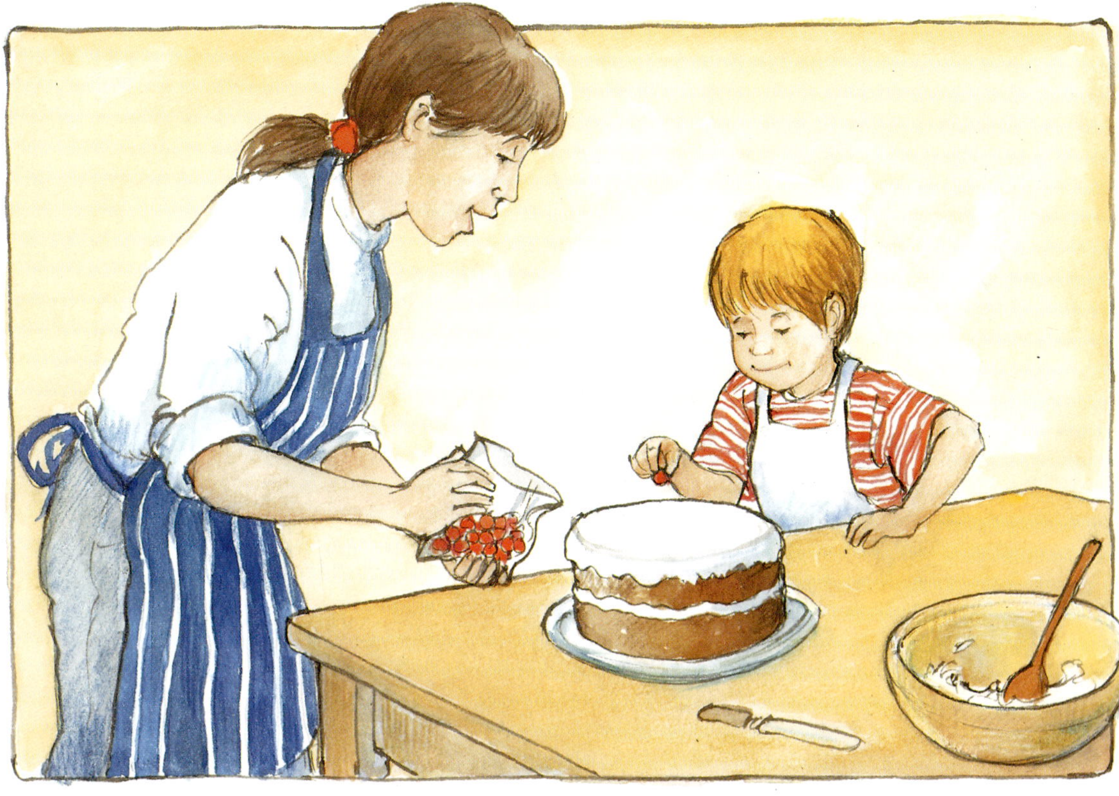

"It's a big cake," said Ben.

"Thanks for helping me, Ben," said Mom.
"Here are some red cherries to go on the top."

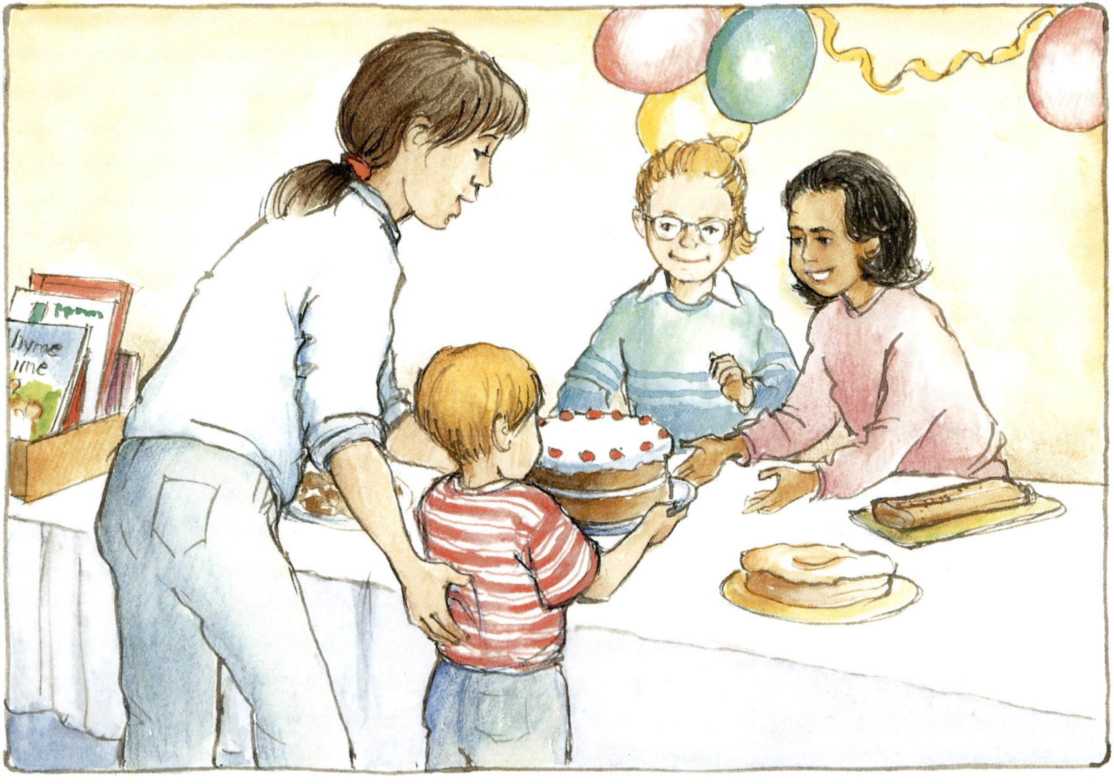

They went to the school fair in the car, and they went inside with the cake.

"Here you are," said Ben. "Here's a **big** cake."

"Thank you," said the girls.

Ben looked at the cakes.
He looked at
Mom's big cake
with the red cherries,
and he looked at
the little brown cakes.

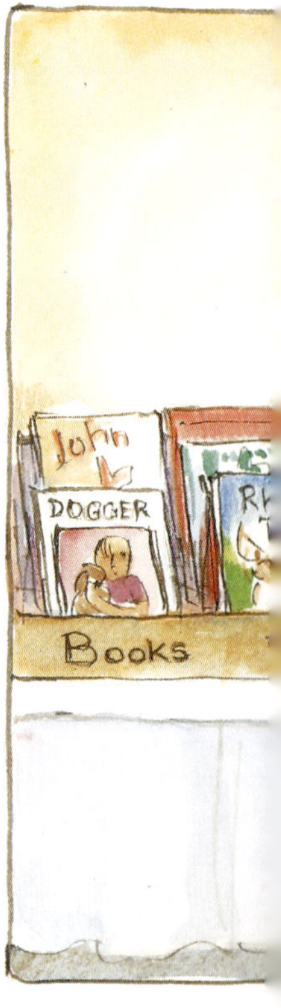
John
DOGGER
Books

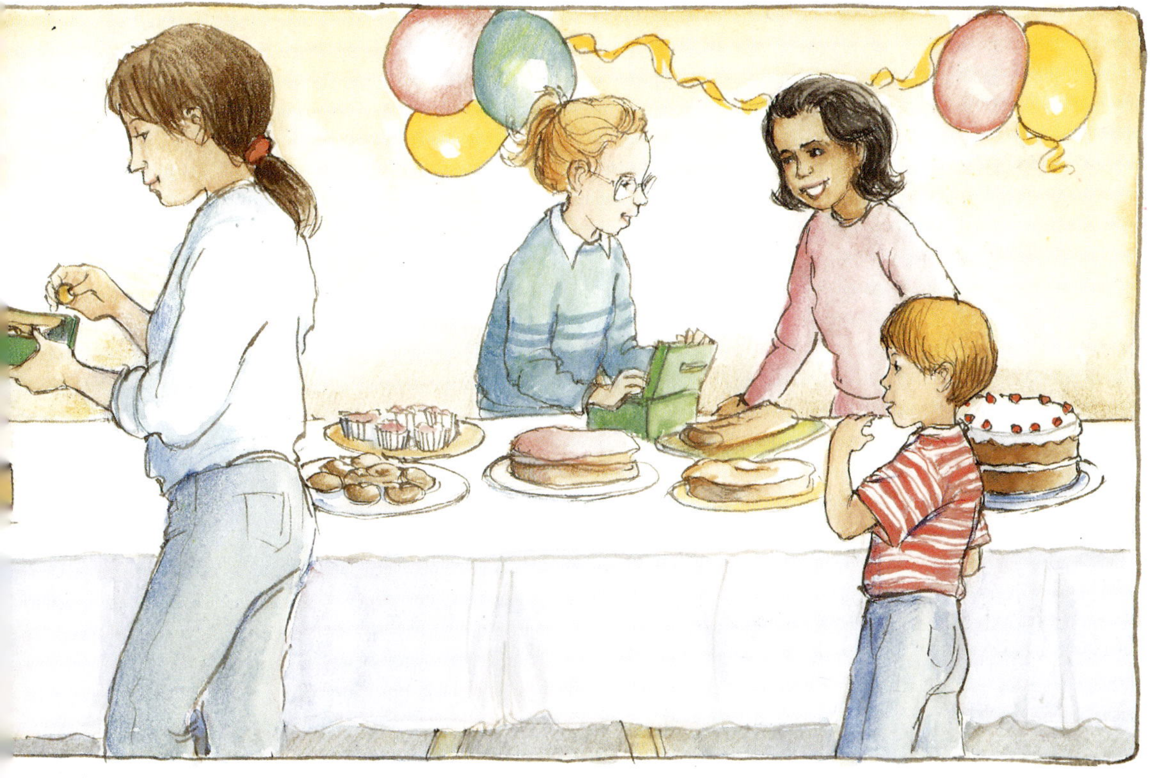

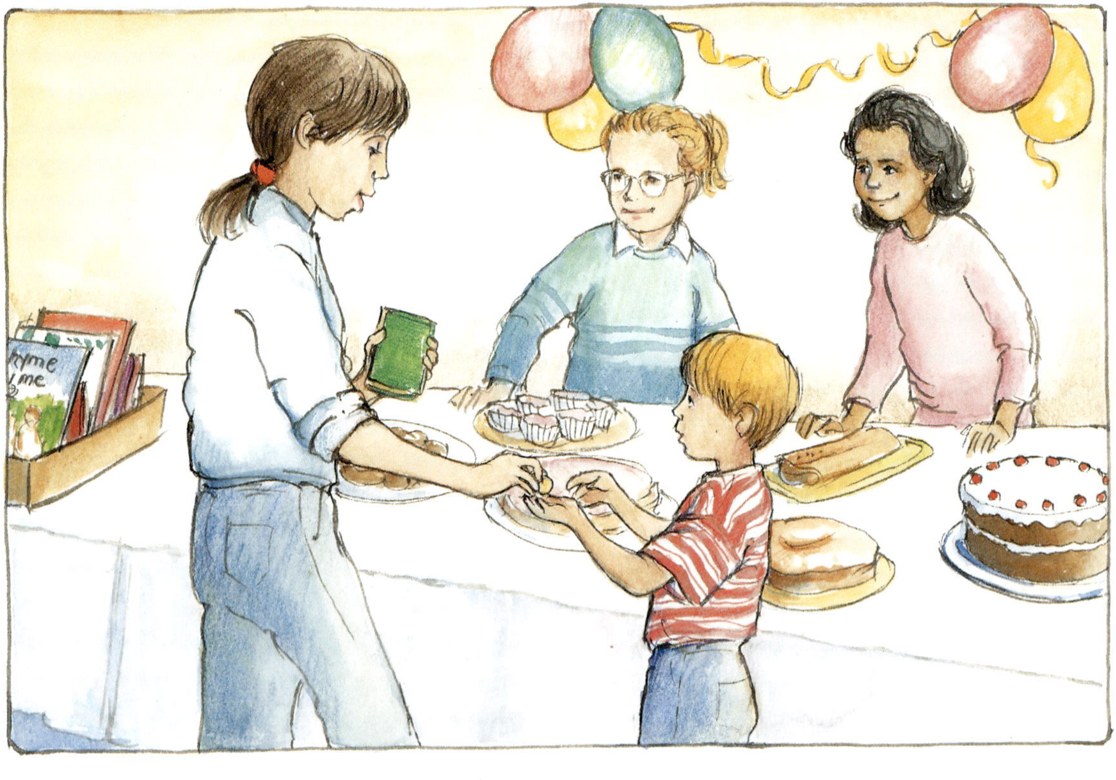

hyme
me

"Ben, please get a cake for us," said Mom.
"I'm going to look at the books."

Ben looked
at all the cakes again ...

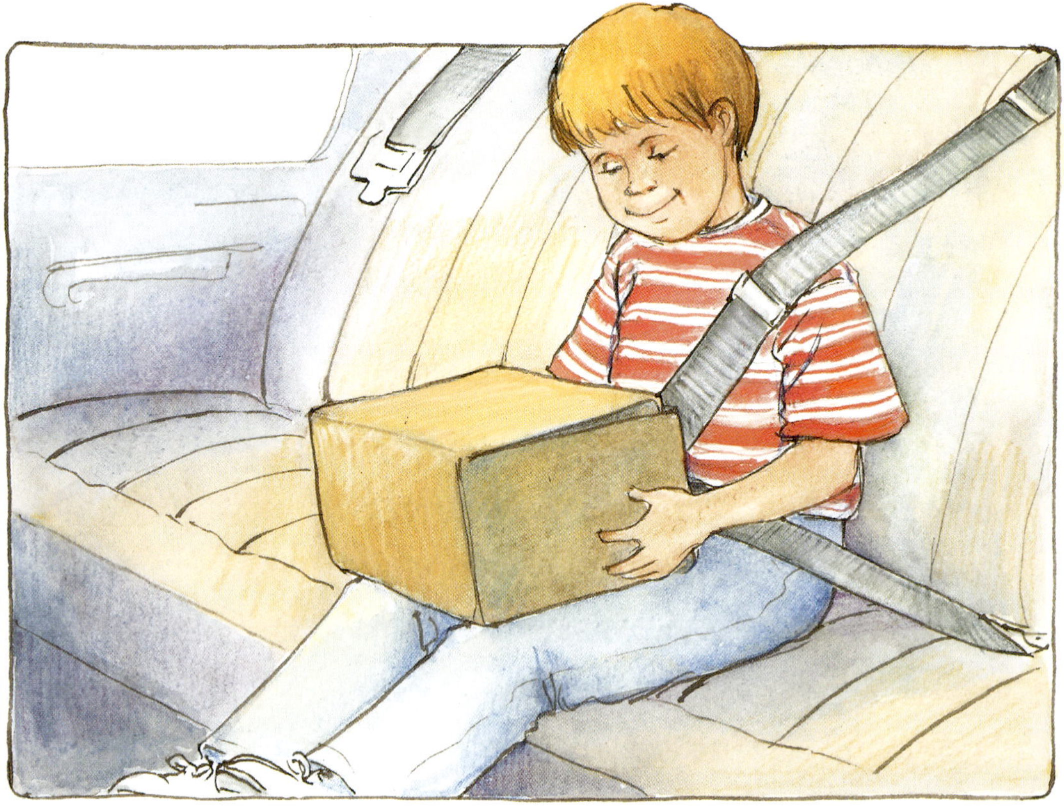

Ben and Mom went home in the car.

Ben took care of the cake.

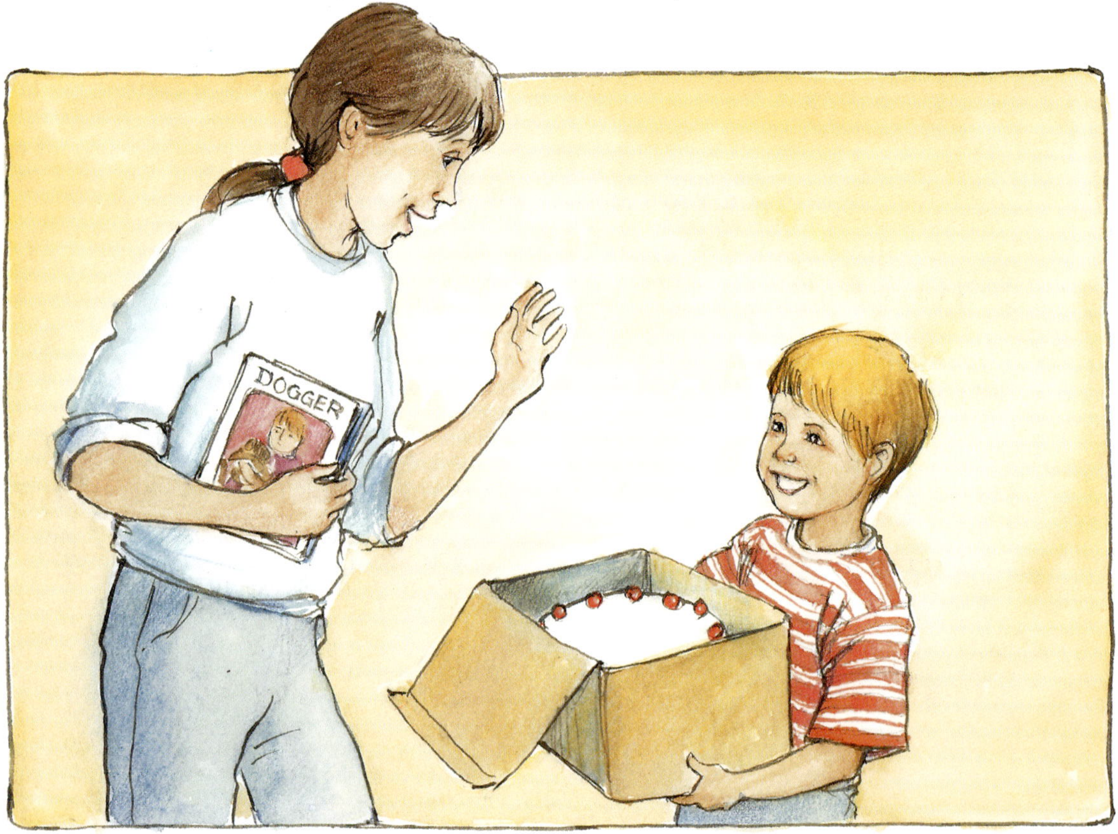
DOGGER

Ben opened the box.
"Here you are, Mom," he said.
"Look!
I got the **best** cake for you.
I got the best cake
at the fair."

"I'm hungry," said Ben.

"Let's have some," said Mom.

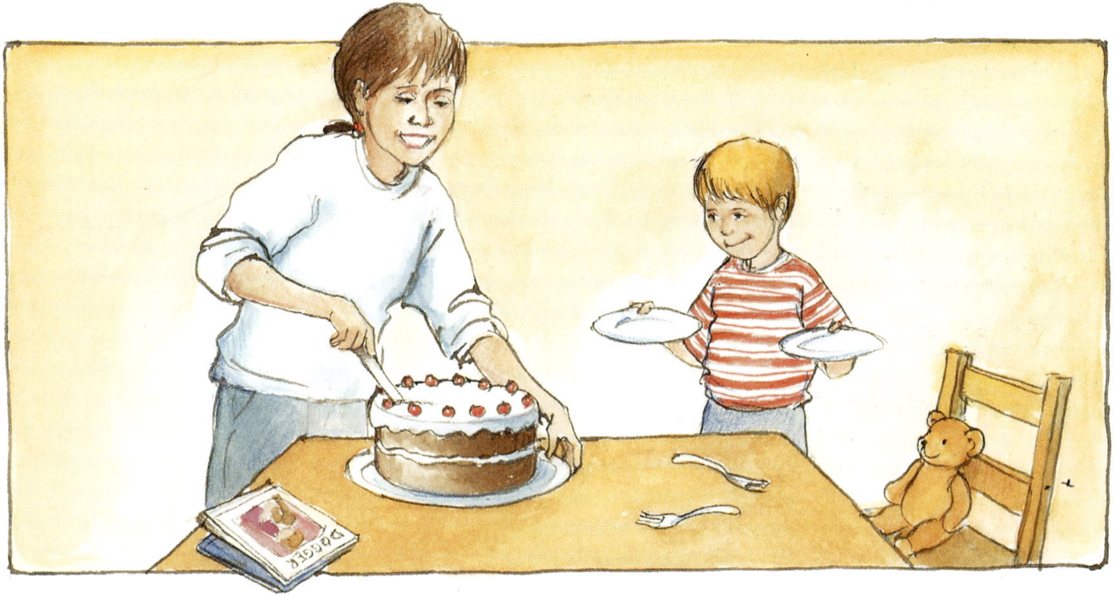

Rigby Platinum PMs
Blue Level

U.S. Edition © 2006
Harcourt Achieve Inc.
10801 N. MoPac Expressway
Building #3
Austin, TX 78759
www.harcourtachieve.com

Text © 1994 Beverley Randell
Illustrations © 2005 Thomson Learning Australia
Originally published in Australia by Thomson Learning Australia

All rights reserved. No part of the material protected by this copyright may be reproduced
or utilized in any form or by any means, in whole or in part, without permission in
writing from the copyright owner. Requests for permission should be mailed to:
Copyright Permissions, Harcourt Achieve Inc., P.O. Box 27010, Austin, Texas 78755.

Rigby and Steck-Vaughn are trademarks of Harcourt Achieve Inc. registered in
the United States of America and/or other jurisdictions.

10 9 8 7 6 5 4 3 2 1
09 08 07 06 05

Printed and bound in China by 1010 Printing Limited

The best cake
ISBN 1-4189-0086-9

Platinum Edition

1
2
3
4
5
6
7
8
9
10
11
12
13
14
15
16
17
18
19
20
21
22
23
24

Blue Level 10

Rigby PM Collection Platinum Edition

Harcourt Achieve
Rigby • Saxon • Steck-Vaughn

ISBN 1-4189-0086-9
90
9 781418 900861

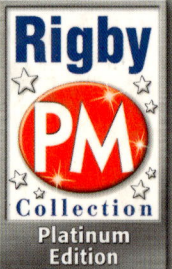

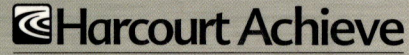